Travel Through Time
Making Waves

Water Travel Past and Present

Jane Shuter

Raintree

Chicago, Illinois

© 2004 Raintree
Published by Raintree, a division of Reed Elsevier, Inc.
Chicago, IL 60602
Customer Service 888-363-4266
Visit our website at www.raintreelibrary.com

For more information address the publisher:
Raintree, 100 N. LaSalle, Suite 1200, Chicago IL 60602

Printed and bound in China by the South China Printing Company.

08 07 06 05 04
10 9 8 7 6 5 4 3 2 1

Library of Congress Cataloging-in-Publication Data:

Shuter, Jane.
  Travel by sea / Jane Shuter.
    p. cm. -- (Travel through time)
Includes bibliographical references and index.
Contents: Over the water -- Early boats -- Empire building -- Crossing the ocean -- Trading and settling -- Finding new lands -- Canals -- Sail versus steam -- Riverboats -- Working steamers -- Passenger steamships -- Modern ships.
  ISBN 1-4109-0581-0 (hc) 1-4109-0980-8 (pb)
  1. Boats and boating--Juvenile literature. 2. Ships--Juvenile literature. 3. Navigation--Juvenile literature. 4. Ocean travel--Juvenile literature. [1. Boats and boating--History. 2. Ships--History. 3. Transportation--History.] I. Title. II. Series: Shuter, Jane. Travel through time.
  VM150.S58 2004
  623.8--dc21

                    2003010203

Acknowledgments
The publishers would like to thank the following for permission to reproduce photographs:p. 4 Hulton Archive; p. 5, 21, 23, 25, 29 Corbis; p. 6 J. Leipe/Photo Archive; p. 7 Nick Wheeler/Corbis; pp. 8, 12, 24 AKG; p. 9 British Museum; p. 10 Popperfoto; p. 11 National Museum of Denmark; p. 13 Science and Society Picture Library; pp. 14, 18 Mary Evans Picture Library; p. 16 Bridgeman Art Library; p. 17 Bettmann/Corbis; p. 19 National Maritime Museum; p. 20 Museum of the City of New York/Corbis; p. 22 Illustrate London News Picture Library; p. 26 Najlah Feanny/Corbis; p. 27 Pete Trafford/Corbis; p. 28 Pete Tafford/ATM.

Cover photograph of a 1930s travel poster for Cunard Cruise ships reproduced with permission of Advertising Archives.

Every effort has been made to contact copyright holders of any material reproduced in this book. Any omissions will be rectified in subsequent printings if notice is given to the publishers.

Contents

Over the Water 4

Early Boats 6

Empire Building 8

The Vikings 10

Trading and Settling 12

Finding New Lands 14

Canals 16

From Sail to Steam 18

Riverboats 20

Working Steamships 22

Passenger Steamships 24

Modern Ships 26

Into the Future 28

Find Out for Yourself 30

Glossary 31

Index 32

Any words appearing in bold, **like this,** are explained in the Glossary.

Over the Water

People have always wanted to use oceans and rivers to move around. Boats can take people farther and faster than walking. They can also carry much more weight than a person or animal, and so they can be used to carry heavy loads from place to place.

Oceans and rivers are not just used for travel. Fish has always been an important food and boats help fishers go farther for more fish and different kinds of fish.

The manner of their fishing.

A Cannow

John White made this drawing of Native Americans fishing in 1584.

4

Homes on water

People have sometimes built their homes on islands in lakes or **lagoons.** They moved around by canoe. In the 1300s the Aztecs of Central America built two settlements on Lake Texcoco. The lake kept them safe from enemies.

HOW FAST?

The earliest sailors could only move as fast as they could paddle. Over 4,000 years ago, an ancient Egyptian is said to have paddled a reed boat about 3 to 6 miles (5 to 10 kilometers) in an hour. In about 3100 B.C.E. people began to use sails . This made travel twice as fast, or more with a good wind. A modern sailing boat can reach speeds of about 30 miles (48 kilometers) per hour.

Venice, Italy, is a city built on a lagoon. Today most people move around the city on *vaporetti*, which are bus boats.

Early Boats

Early peoples built simple boats that were small and light, with low sides. Light boats were easy to steer but also turned over easily in rough water. So early sailors stayed close to land, where the water was often calmer.

MAKING A BOAT

The earliest boats were probably made over 5,000 years ago from natural **materials** that rotted and left nothing behind. In places with plenty of trees, people **hollowed** out logs for boats. In places with few trees, they used bundles of reeds tied together. From about 3000 B.C.E. people sewed animal skins together around a wooden boat frame, or filled them with air, so they would float.

This is a model of an ancient Egyptian boat made from reeds.

Finding their way

Early sailors had no maps or **compasses** to help them **navigate** (find their way). They had to stay close to land. If they did this, they could watch the land for things they recognized, like a hill or a river going inland. As time passed, people made better boats. They added sails from about 3100 B.C.E. These caught the wind to make the boats go faster. They used an oar at the back to help steer.

The people of Iraq have never changed the **design** of their boats, because they work well and are cheap to build.

Empire Building

The ancient Phoenicians, Romans, and Greeks all lived around the Mediterranean Sea at different times from about 1000 B.C.E. to about C.E. 300. They built **empires** by taking over more and more land from other people. They needed two different kinds of boat for empire building.

Warships

Ships for fighting had to be fast and easy to steer. They had to carry a lot of soldiers, who rowed the ship and fought at sea. Warships had rows of oars on both sides and not much space for anything else.

This is a Roman carving of trading ships coming into port.

Trading ships

Trading ships were bigger, heavier, and slower. They had a lot of space for the **goods** and people they moved around the empires. Ships that sailed in the Atlantic Ocean were made from thick oak and had sails made from animal skins. They needed to be strong to cope with stormy weather.

This painting on an ancient Greek cup shows pirates, on the right, attacking a trading ship.

PYTHIAS THE GREEK

Pythias the Greek sailed from the south of France (then in the Greek Empire) to Britain and on to Iceland 2,300 years ago. He sailed on trading boats and in small light ships that stayed close to land. Compared to the Mediterranean Sea, he found the **currents** and waves of the Atlantic Ocean amazingly fierce.

The Vikings

The Vikings lived in Scandinavia, in northern Europe. There were so many of them they needed more land and food. So the Vikings sailed off, first to **trade** with, or steal from, other lands and then to live there. They moved south across Europe, east into Russia and west to Iceland, Greenland, and North America.

DIFFERENT BOATS

Viking longboats were used for fighting. They were long and sat higher in the water than earlier ships. This meant they could sail close to the shore and up shallow rivers to attack. They had no decks, just room for a lot of rowers, who were also fighters. Viking trading ships were called knörrs.

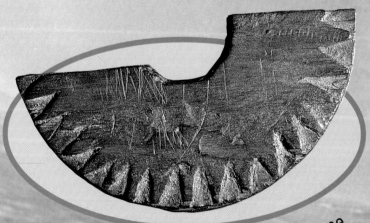

Vikings used **compasses** like this one to help them find their way at sea.

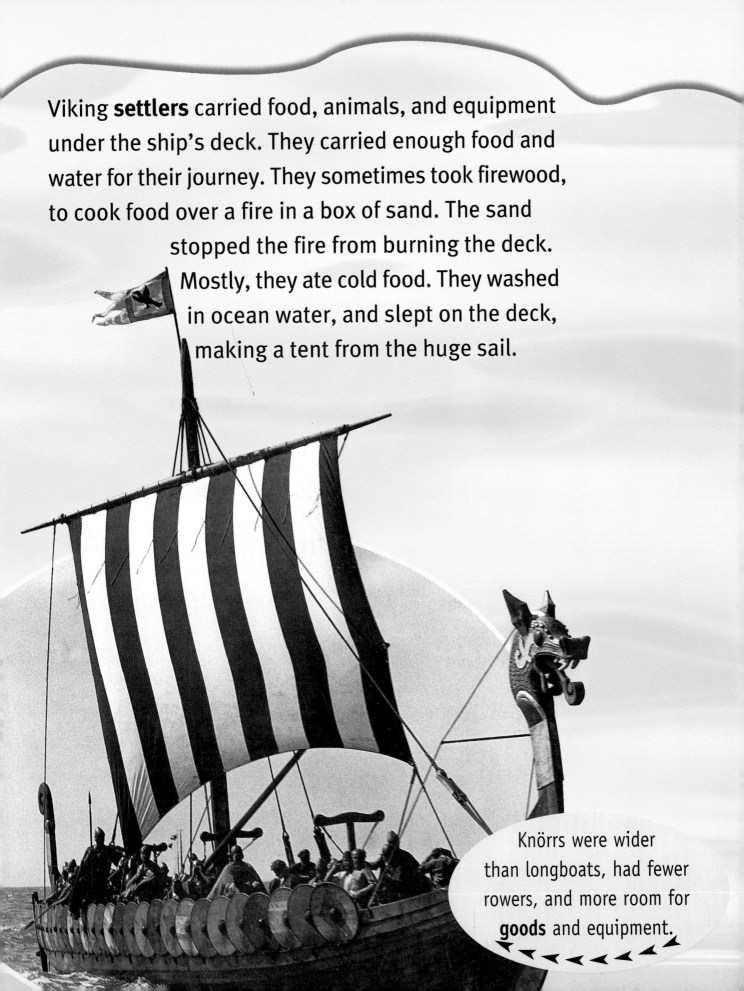

Viking **settlers** carried food, animals, and equipment under the ship's deck. They carried enough food and water for their journey. They sometimes took firewood, to cook food over a fire in a box of sand. The sand stopped the fire from burning the deck. Mostly, they ate cold food. They washed in ocean water, and slept on the deck, making a tent from the huge sail.

Knörrs were wider than longboats, had fewer rowers, and more room for **goods** and equipment.

Trading and Settling

From C.E. 1000, people built bigger ships that could carry far more **goods** and people. These ships were made to sail far across the ocean, out of sight of land. They had to cope with rough weather. People went exploring to find ways by sea instead of long and dangerous land journeys.

Big and Small

People still made small fishing boats and bigger boats to sail close to land. The **design** of these boats stayed the same.

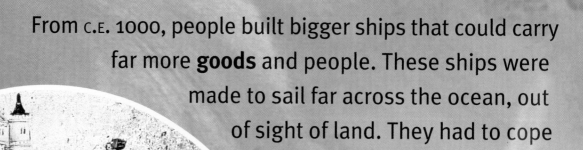

This painting from the 1400s shows small row boats (to travel short distances close to land) and larger ocean-going boats.

Ships that went exploring stayed at sea for a long time. Sailors lived crowded together, with no privacy. They washed in sea water. The food and water they took with them often went bad before the end of their journey. They did not realize that they needed to eat fresh fruit and vegetables to stay healthy, so many became ill.

CROSSING THE SEAS

Some early **inventions** that helped people sail:
- about 2000 B.C.E., ancient Egypt, **rudder**, to steer at sea
- about 300 B.C.E., ancient Greece, astrolabe, to steer by the stars or sun
- C.E. 1300, sea maps marked with **compass** directions

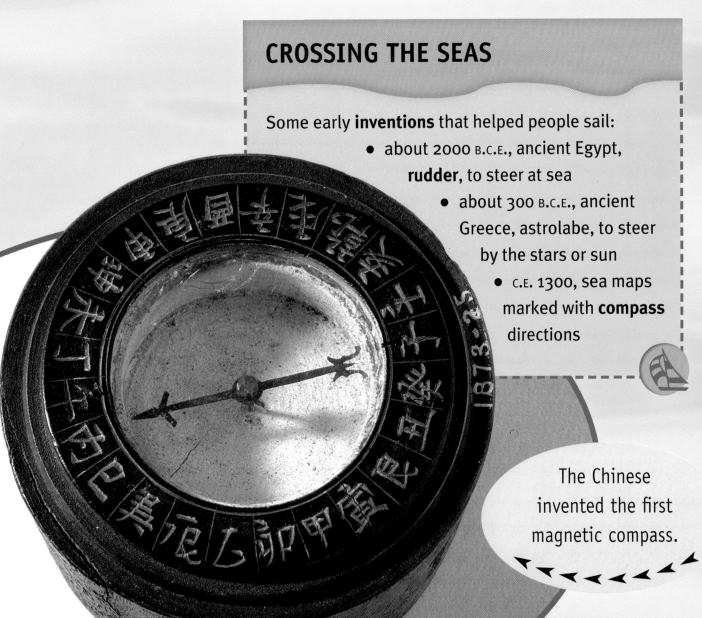

The Chinese invented the first magnetic compass.

Finding New Lands

By c.e. 1500 explorers from Europe had found many different lands. They made careful maps of their travels, which they kept secret. Each country hoped to find treasure. The Spanish who took over parts of South America were soon sending ships full of gold and silver back to Spain. The treasure attracted pirates, who captured the ships and stole everything on board.

Francis Drake sailed around the world in the *Golden Hind*. This painting shows the great ship at sea.

As new lands were discovered, people **emigrated** there. Some of the first European **settlers** of North America traveled there on a ship called the *Mayflower*.

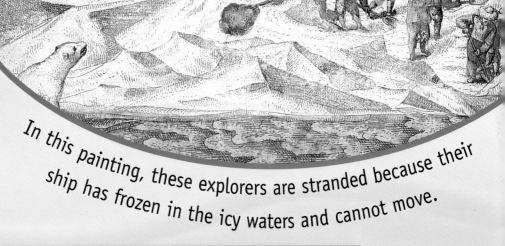

In this painting, these explorers are stranded because their ship has frozen in the icy waters and cannot move.

GOING FURTHER

Some famous explorers and their adventures:

- 1492 Christopher Columbus crossed the Atlantic to America
- 1519–1522 One of five ships led by Ferdinand Magellan sails around the world. Of 234 men only 18 came back. Magellan died.
- 1577–1580 Francis Drake sails around the world
- 1584 Sir Walter Raleigh sends settlers to Virginia

Canals

Rivers and the ocean do not always go where people want to go. So people began to dig their own waterways, called **canals**. When roads were just dirt and stone it was easier to carry heavy loads by water. The **Sumerians** built a canal nearly 100 miles (160 kilometers) long in 2400 B.C.E.

An explosion of canals

The biggest problem with canals was going uphill. By C.E. 1700 people had solved this problem by building locks. Locks are boat-sized "steps" with gates at either end. They are slowly filled with water or emptied, depending on whether a boat is going up or down the hill.

These boats are going into a lock near London, England.

Canals across narrow pieces of land can be useful short cuts. One famous canal is the Panama Canal (built 1907–1914) joining the Atlantic and Pacific Oceans. After this canal was built, people no longer had to sail all the way around South America to get from one ocean to the other.

The Erie Canal in New York was finished in 1825. It joined the Atlantic Ocean to the Great Lakes.

THE BEST WAY TO GO?

Canals were better and cheaper than roads for carrying heavy **goods,** such as coal. Canal travel was slow though, and canals were difficult and expensive to build. Roads began to improve and railroads were **invented.** Heavy goods could now go more easily and cheaply by land, and people stopped building canals.

From Sail to Steam

In 1800, all ships were made from wood and sailed by wind power. Then, **steam power** was **invented.** In 1807 Robert Fulton launched the *Clermont,* the first reliable steamship. Sailing ships, especially "clipper" ships, were faster and more reliable than early steamships.

Clipper ships had many more sails than early sailing ships, to use the wind as much as possible.

SAIL OR STEAM?

In the 1830s sailing ships took about 32 days to cross the Atlantic Ocean. If the winds were poor, it took longer. A steamship took 20 days or less. Changes in design made steamships more and more **efficient.** By 1850 it took 14 days to cross the Atlantic, by 1900 it took just 5 days.

Early steamships had **design** problems. Their engines used a lot of coal and often broke down. Most had sails as well, to use if the engine failed or they ran out of coal. The first regular service across the Atlantic Ocean was run by four ships of the Cunard line. They carried mail and up to 63 passengers. The trip took fourteen days.

In 1838 the *Sirius* was the first ship to cross from Ireland to New York using just steam power. It took eighteen days, ten hours and ran out of coal. The sailors had to burn everything wooden to get there.

Riverboats

Riverboats had different problems than ocean ships. Sailors did not lose sight of land, but they had to worry about changes in the river. Some wide, slow rivers, like the Mississippi, had shifting banks of sandy **silt** that a boat could easily get stuck on.

By the 1880s Mississippi steamships were luxurious, with lots of food, drink, and entertainment for the passengers.

Steamboats on the Mississippi

Paddle steamboats were used on many rivers from the 1830s. They provided a nicer choice to the dirty and dangerous journey by land. They also carried heavy loads, such as cotton, from big farms in the south.

Rivers all over the world were busy with lots of different boats. While paddle steamboats were sailing the Mississippi, the Yangtze (now called the Chang) River in China was full of sampans, **barges,** and sailing ships.

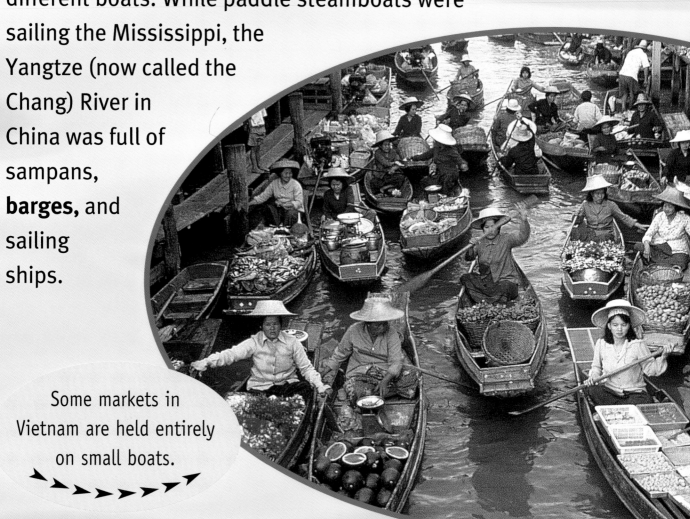

Some markets in Vietnam are held entirely on small boats.

SAMPANS

Sampans are small Chinese riverboats that have been in use for over a thousand years. They are small boats, with a covered part at the back to shelter people and **goods.** Modern sampans often have engines. Before this, they were rowed or pushed along with a long pole and steered by a long oar at the back.

Working Steamships

By the 1890s almost all **cargo** ships were steamships. They were very reliable, unlike early steamships. They had better engines that burned far less coal. The ship's main body, called the **hull,** was made from a new metal, steel. It was much stronger than wood.

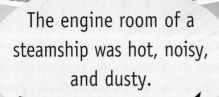

The engine room of a steamship was hot, noisy, and dusty.

BETTER STEAMSHIPS

These **inventions** helped steamships to go farther, faster, and more cheaply:

- 1836 propellers invented, stronger and more efficient than paddles
- 1840s iron hulls used, stronger than wooden ones
- 1870s steel hulls used, strong and lighter than iron ones
- 1884 turbine engine invented, used steam more efficiently to make a cheaper, powerful engine

Working steamships laid underwater **telegraph** cables across the Atlantic Ocean and to Australia. Steamships carried mail and **goods** around the world. They got so big that small steamships, called tugs, had to "tug" them up rivers and into ports.

Busy ports

The noisy docks of ports like London were crammed with ships and warehouses. Different goods unloaded in different parts of the docks. You could tell where you were by sniffing and smelling tea, spices, or fruit!

In the 1880s special refrigerated ships were built to take meat around the world. They kept the meat cold and stopped it from going bad.

Passenger Steamships

The passenger ships of the 1850s carried animals to feed the passengers fresh meat along the way. Passengers had cabins to sleep in, but had to wash in sea water.

Big improvements

By the early 1900s, the ships, especially ocean liners crossing the Atlantic Ocean, were very luxurious. The *Titanic*, built in 1912, even had steam baths and its own telephone system.

The Titanic took less than three hours to sink.

UNSINKABLE?

The *Titanic* was called "unsinkable." On its first crossing from Southampton to New York, in 1912, it hit an iceberg and sank. Over half of the 2,340 passengers and crew on board died.

Disasters like the sinking of the *Titanic* made governments make stricter safety rules for passenger ships. Disasters did not stop people from traveling on these ships. They were the only way at the time to travel the world.

Only for the rich?

Prices for journeys depended on how many people you shared a cabin with and if you had meals. Poor people could travel in "steerage," crowded together in the most unpleasant parts of the ship with no meals or running water. This was the way many people **emigrated** from Europe to the United States in the early 1900s.

In the 1930s, posters such as this one made travel by ocean liner seem like a grand adventure.

Modern Ships

From 1945 onward ships have used modern technology to go farther faster. They are also sailed by fewer sailors. Diesel engines, first used in ships in 1902, became much more **efficient** and took over from steam ones. Ships can carry far heavier loads than airplanes. **Cargo** ships now often carry the **goods** in large metal containers on the deck and below deck.

Tankers

There are also ships to carry just liquids, such as oil. They are called tankers. However, if these oil tankers have an accident the spilled oil causes terrible **pollution.**

These firefighters are trying to stop a blaze that has started after an oil spill.

New **inventions,** like **sonar** and **radar,** mean ships can travel in bad weather more easily. They use radios and computers to keep in touch with other ships and with people on shore.

This hovercraft is coming into land.

NEW WAYS OF TRAVELING AT SEA

New inventions created new ways of traveling by sea:

- 1956 Hydrofoils used metal "foils" underneath that act like water skis
- 1968 Hovercraft hovered just above the surface of the water on a cushion of air
- 1975 Jetfoils are hydrofoils driven by a jet of water pushed out of the back

Into the Future

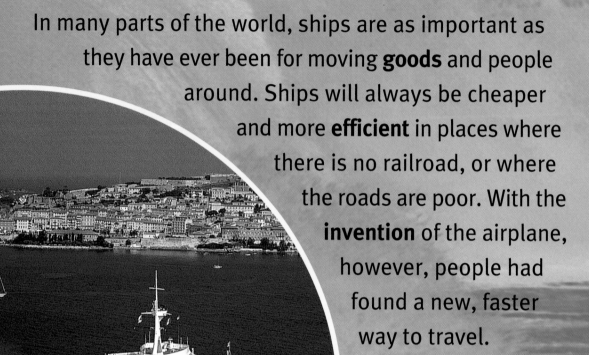

In many parts of the world, ships are as important as they have ever been for moving **goods** and people around. Ships will always be cheaper and more **efficient** in places where there is no railroad, or where the roads are poor. With the **invention** of the airplane, however, people had found a new, faster way to travel.

Saving time

Planes save time. As soon as they were comfortable enough, more people used them to travel. Passenger ships are now mainly used for vacation cruises.

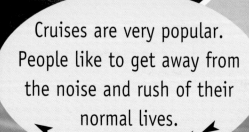

Cruises are very popular. People like to get away from the noise and rush of their normal lives.

Ships will always be useful for transporting heavy goods and for fishing. The rising cost of oil means that ship **designers** need to look for a new fuel to power them. Transporting goods on oil-powered ships is getting too expensive.

Oil-powered ships also cause **pollution** if they have an accident. The Japanese are trying new fuels. One example is a magnet-driven ship, *Yamato I*.

YAMATO I

Magnets surround a water-filled pipe under *Yamato I*. Electricity is passed through it. This pushes the water out, hard enough to make the ship move.

Huge ships, such as this one, will still be used to carry heavy goods around the world.

Find Out for Yourself

You can find out more about the history of sea travel by talking to adults about how travel has changed during their lifetimes. Your local library will have books about this, too. You will find the answers to many of your questions in this book, but you can also use other books and the Internet.

Books to read

Oxlade, Chris. *Transport Around the World: Boats and Ships*. Chicago: Heinemann Library, 2001.

Parker, Vic. *Speedy Machines: Boats*. London: Belitha Press, 1999.

Using the Internet

Explore the Internet to find out more about water travel. Websites can change, but if one of the links below no longer works, don't worry. Use a search engine, such as www.yahooligans.com or www.internet4kids.com, and type in keywords such as "longboat," "canal," and *Yamato I*."

Websites

http://www.bbc.co.uk/schools/vikings/travel/index.shtml
Find out more about Viking ships and sailors.

http://www.mariner.org
Discover galleries filled with an international collection of detailed ship models, paintings, arts, and other seafaring artifacts.

Glossary

barge boat with a wide, flat bottom, to go up shallow rivers and canals

canal waterway made by people

cargo things carried on a ship or other vehicle

compass object used to find your way

design to think of a way of making something to do a certain job

empire all the lands controlled by one country

emigrate to leave one country to go live in another one

goods things that are made, bought, and sold

hull frame of a ship

invent make or discover something for the first time

lagoon water close to land partly cut off from the ocean by a long strip of sand

navigate to find the way from one place to another

pollution causing damage to the natural world, making it dirty, messy, and often dangerous for living things

radar when radio waves are bounced off objects to locate them

rudder oar at the back of a ship that moves to change the direction of the ship

settler person who moves from one place to live in another

silt fine mud, sand, or soil that is moved around on a river bed as the river flows

sonar when sound waves are bounced off objects to locate them

steam power power made by burning coal under a sealed tank of water to create steam

telegraph a machine that sends electronic messages over wires

trade buying and selling, or swapping, things

ex

astrolabe	13	ocean liners	24, 25
barges	16, 21	oil-powered ships	26, 29
bus boats	5	paddle steamers	20, 21
canals	16–17	Panama Canal	17
canoes	5	passenger ships	19, 24–25, 28
cargo ships	4, 17, 20, 22, 23, 26, 29	pirates	9, 14
		ports	23
clipper ships	18	propellers	22
compasses	7, 11, 13	Pythias the Greek	9
cruises	28	radar	27
diesel engines	26	reed boats	5, 6
early boats	5, 6–7	refrigerated ships	23
exploration	12, 13, 14–15	riverboats	20–21
fishing boats	4, 12	rudders	13
hovercraft	27	sailing boats and ships	5, 7, 8, 18, 21
hulls	22	sampans	21
hydrofoils	27	sonar	27
jetfoils	27	steamships	18–19, 20, 22–25
knörrs	10	steering	7, 13, 21
locks	16	tankers	26
longboats	10	*Titanic*	24, 25
magnet-driven ships	29	trading ships	9, 10
modern ships	26–29	tugs	23
navigation	7, 11, 13	turbine engines	22
		Vikings	10–11
		warships	8